BUSINESS HABITS

LEADERSHIP SECRETS THAT

LEAD TO BETTER RESULTS

By K. Connors

Table of Contents

Introduction

Great leaders jump out of their environment and are determined to do something different, something more important, than just being a manager. They motivate, inspire, and drive change. The way to keep inspiration is to give it away. The way to have a great leadership personality is to radiate a great leadership personality. One of the great secrets of leadership success is to let your inner light shine. The way to succeed in leadership is to help other people succeed in leadership.

We are encouragement by giving encouragement. Give people you lead your best, and their best comes back to you. Our leadership abilities are developed, our talents multiplied, and all of the joy and success of great leadership are ours because of what we have given away. Great leadership comes as a reward for what we have done for others.

Take time to be successful, to be kind, to be considerate, to motivate, inspire, and drive change. With determination and vision, motivate the people and reach for things worthwhile. You know what will happen. The result is sure. Every day will be a day of glory, and you will become a great leader. One great lesson we should all learn is to see the possibilities in ourselves and in others. It is satisfying to see other people climb higher through our assistance. It is better to be a burst of sunshine than a wet sponge.

Cease to prepare, and you cease to grow; cease to grow, and you will cease to be a great leader. It is absolutely certain that the only people who can ever become great leaders are the people who can hold out, who can bide their time, who understand that patience is a teacher. It was Washington's patience, as much as his military genius, that won the Revolution. It was the patience of Robert Kahn and Vint Cerf that gave us the internet, and the patience of Columbus that discovered a new world.

The idea that everything worth doing was intended for someone more capable is what keeps the average manager from becoming a great leader. First, lead yourself to greater things today than you did yesterday. Forget those who envy you, those who would pull you down and trample you under their feet, hoping to gain a foothold for themselves.

There is a personal price that a person must pay for being a great leader. Every great leader must make a fight for the truth within themselves. Vision and integrity are the food upon which leadership thrives. It is vision, integrity, and the will of the spirit that makes great leaders. These great leaders manage the great organizations of the world, and build monuments of achievement that reach to the very stars.

Whether in a political campaign or leading a movement for civic righteousness, the amount of work involved is almost inconceivable, and the leader's influence is as wide as the earth itself. Great leaders stand tall like a giant mountain high above the storms that keep little managers in a daily state of turmoil.

The real difference between those who succeed and those who don not is, one thinks they can, the other thinks they cannot. One discovers their leadership greatness, the other does not. One learns that they can be a great leader, and the idea of being a great leader motivates and inspires them. The other one thinks that all of the great things in the world were intended for someone else.

Leadership success must come as the result of one's own efforts, and not at the expense of someone else. Successful organizations are seldom built up by tearing down other people. When a leader allows deceit to become a part of their working capital, all that is noble in them withers and dies.

So what are their secrets to leadership? Are leaders born with this trait or do they develop it themselves? Continue to read and judge for yourself.

Being Proactive

When one assumes a position of leadership, he must determine for himself what type of leader he chooses to become. Will he decide to be just another space holder? Or will he proactively pursue the best possible course of action by strategically, thoroughly considering, and evaluating his choices of action plans and articulating his perspectives and points of view in a way which motivates stakeholders to care more and to get more involved? In my four decades of identifying, qualifying, training, developing, and consulting to thousands of actual, and/ or potential leaders, I've learned, the vast majority of those, in these positions, choose to limit their possibilities, by remaining within the confines of their comfort zone. The greatest leaders, however, expand their possibilities, opting for superior, proactive leadership. This chapter will address the secrets of proactive leaders.

1.   Proactive leaders are cautious without becoming paralyzed by the potential downside of action. They pursue their goals continuously but incrementally, testing and evaluating progress toward the goal. This approach assures movement toward the goal without exposing the organization to unnecessary and avoidable jeopardy. They don't play it safe, but do play it cautiously.

2.   Proactive leaders focus most of their time and energy on organizational stability and goal attainment. They minimize time and energy absorbed by worrying about unlikely contingencies and maintaining the status quo.

3.   Proactive leaders make decisions and take action thoughtfully but quickly. They do not delay or postpone decisions or actions, try to avoid or defer doing what needs done, and they do not hesitate or proceed reluctantly. Their actions and reactions are not impulsive or ill considered. They are, instead, decisive and timely.

4.   Proactive leaders do not shirk or avoid responsibility and have little tolerance for people who do. They are committed to the welfare of the organization and to its mission. From the perspective of personal responsibility, they do everything they have agreed to do to the best of their ability and accept additional responsibility to the extent necessary to assure the organization's success. They may decide that they are unwilling or unable to continue accepting the responsibilities they have agreed to accept. In that event, they will be up-front about their decision and in the meantime, they will do what they have agreed to do at the highest level of which they are capable. The organization always gets their best effort.

5.   Proactive leaders take calculated risks and carefully considered chances with hard resources such as capital and soft resources such as political support. Before taking such risks, they

first determine the cost to the organization of paying the hard or soft resource bill if their action is unsuccessful. Next, they determine the extent of total organizational resource reduction that could result from having to pay that bill. How much worse off would the organization be if the bill is paid? That is "X" or the downside cost of action. "Y" or the upside benefit of action is similarly calculated in terms of the level of increase in total hard and soft resources if the action is successful. Action then gambles "X" against the possibility of "Y." Two additional factors are then considered: the likelihood of getting "Y," and how much the value of "Y" exceeds the value of "X." They do not gamble a lot to only gain a little.

For the proactive leader, then, taking calculated risks with organizational resources means that the potential value of attaining "Y" justifies the risk of having to pay the downside bill "X." In either event, contingency plans are in place to manage the outcome.

6.   Proactive leaders have a high tolerance for and acceptance of differing personalities, traits and characteristics, personal styles, individual values and beliefs, and for the idiosyncrasies of people. Similarly, they easily manage fluctuations in people's moods, points of view, and interests. Alternatively, they have little tolerance for sub-standard work, less than complete attention to the task at hand, or lackluster performance. They always give their best effort and expect others to do the same.

7.   Proactive leaders expect others to do things correctly, to give everything they do their best effort, to succeed. They are surprised when people make mistakes, give things less than their best effort and do not succeed. Since they expect success, they assume personal responsibility for the mistakes of others, lackluster effort, non-success. Their first take on the situation is that they haven't been smart enough or skilled enough to effectuate the right outcome. They then work with the person to identify the deficiencies, to modify their (the proactive leader's) performance so that they better facilitate the person's success. Of course, the proactive leader occasionally determines that a specific person either cannot or will not perform as expected no matter what is done but typically, the proactive leader assumes shared responsibility for assuring the success of others.

8.   Proactive leaders accept people as is. Their goal is not to change anyone. Rather, they focus on encouraging and facilitating in ways that enable each person to achieve optimal performance within the context of their skills, abilities, and interests. Concurrently, they expect people to expand and improve their capacities and are ready to help with that process however they can, within the resources and constraints of the organization. People aren't expected to change but are expected to grow and develop as organizational participants.

9.   Proactive leaders aren't stingy with praise nor are they lavish with it. They are quick to recognize and acknowledge the successes and accomplishments of others but don't confuse praise with simple good manners. Please and thank you and noting that someone did a good job or was helpful are not examples of praise. They are, rather, merely examples of good manners and are integral to the proactive leader's habitual deportment. Alternatively, praise is an intentional and thoughtful action which privately or publicly acknowledges and commends excellence. Proactive leaders reserve praise for exceptional or extraordinary performance, never missing an opportunity to praise when individual or group performance meets that standard.

10.   Proactive leaders understand that holding people responsible and accountable on the one hand and blaming and accusing them on the other are not the same. Holding someone responsible is a performance standard. Holding them accountable is a performance expectation. Alternatively, blaming and accusing imply negative opinions and perceptions of the individual. To blame someone or accuse them represents a pejorative assessment of them. Blaming and accusing are always subjective and personal while responsibility and accountability are performance elements that can be objectively evaluated and, if necessary, adjusted. Since the individual or group are accountable for their performance, the level of responsibility extended to them may be increased or

decreased, depending on their performance. To blame or accuse are counterproductive and incompatible with proactive leadership. Holding people responsible and accountable are key elements in the proactive leader's approach with people. It starts with holding himself (or herself) responsible and accountable and then simply extending the principle to everyone else in the organization.

11.	Proactive leaders resist the temptation to either focus on what is not going well or on what is. It may be a function of human nature to attend mostly to the negative or to the positive, depending on one's personality. Proactive leaders understand that this is not a simple matter of choice or personal preference. The key to success is seeing that neither focusing on the positive nor on the negative is advisable. At a more fundamental level, the reality is that the organization is continuously transitioning from a past state to a future state. The primary responsibility of the proactive leader is to affect the transition so as to actualize the desired future state. To do this, the task is to reduce and eliminate the disparity between the present and future states, without redefining or compromising the future state. Focus then needs to be collectively on the cluster of elements that affect the future state either as contributors or as detractors, understanding that neither is more or less important than the other. Focus must be on the result.

12.	Proactive leaders demonstrate their respect for and are pleased by, the successes and accomplishments of others. The key here is twofold. They both respect the achievements of others and actively demonstrate that respect and the pleasure they experience when others do well. Respect in this context includes holding the person and the action or accomplishment in high esteem, feeling delighted, and actively expressing approval.

Much as in life, it is about the choices we make. Will you opt for proactive leadership?

Think About The End Goal

Begin with the end in mind is one of "The 7 Habits of Highly Effective People" in the famous Stephen Covey's bestseller. In its most basic form, it refers to always having the image of the end of your life as your frame of reference to evaluate everything else. It is about starting things with a clear idea of your destination, so that the steps you take are always in the right direction. If you have to be busy, at least you should be doing what's important to you.

It is based on the principle that things are created twice. First creation is in your mind and the second is in physical reality. Studies of our Reticular Activating System suggest that when we visualize our goals and are conscious about them, our full energy and personal talents are activated in order to develop them effectively.

Today, this powerful concept is used in many contexts and areas of our lives: leadership, entrepreneurship, project management, sports competition, personal productivity. Coaches teach elite athletes to imagine the successful result of an event before they start competing. If you're sure about how to complete a project, you will be able to plan it efficiently, you will be able to better communicate its purpose to the people involved, you will be able to accurately measure its success upon completion and, above all, you will have the proper motivation to tackle it.

David Allen also supports this concept is his book Getting Things Done. He points out the importance of vision in his natural way of planning projects: "to access the conscious and unconscious resources available to you, you must have a clear picture in your mind of what success should look like". There are three steps to beginning with the end in mind, and I would like to share them with you and explain each one.

1. **Identify Your Organization's Long-Term "Going to the Moon" Goal**

I start my clients with the first component of backward thinking by asking: What is the larger than life, long-term goal of the organization?

For some clients, this can be truly inspirational. It's their "going to the moon" statement. When first vocalized, it will be both terrifying and invigorating. When President John F. Kennedy said the U.S. would land a man safely on the moon, this statement was met with bewildered astonishment. Yet this statement inspired many to pursue careers in science and make President Kennedy's dream a reality.

So, what's your "going to the moon" goal or vision? It should be larger than life. It should be between 5 and 30 years out. And it should be specific, measurable, and inspirationally challenging.

It should evoke a quickness to the heart and an expression of wonder should it be achieved. For example, Coca Cola had the modest goal of putting a Coke within the reach of every human being on the planet, and I think they did pretty well.

2. Envision a Three Year Picture Grounded Upon Your Larger Inspirational Goal

Ask yourself and envision: What are the characteristics of the firm at the end of the next three years?

Paint a brief picture of no more than 15 bullet points, describing what your business will look like. How many employees will you have? What will your facility look like? What new markets will you have entered? What new divisions will have opened? What new software will you have mastered?

Dream out loud and be bold. Imagine you're looking back at the Earth from the moon, and think about how you got there.

3. Determine Your Organization's One Year Plan

What are five to seven key goals for the upcoming 12 months? These specific and measurable targets should focus all your efforts during the next year, and achieving them should support both your 3-year and 10-year goals.

So, consider these three elements as the foundation for some great backward thinking. Starting with the end in mind will provide the crisp clarity and focused execution you need while eliminating the bright, shiny objects that distract every leadership team along the journey. Think backward and don't play small ball.

Prioritizing Your To Do List

Responsibility prioritizing is done by everyone and about everything we undertake. From the smallest effort we exert to the most complicated mission attempted, each receives a position of importance. We decide when and how tasks are completed and the value placed on each one. The list can be written or mental, but it is still made.

Everything about our lives gets prioritized. No matter what we are involved in or tasks we must accomplish, a priority will be set for them all. Often this is done by what we feel is most important or will be due first. Other times they are ordered by the time available to achieve their completion. Most times it seems we are like firemen and only do things when they become an emergency. Whatever criteria we use to determine this list, we need to expect things will occur to interrupt the process but persistence is required to stay on course.

The decision when we perform these duties is our own, but do we use the best process? There have been many proven statements and opinions given as to the most efficient ways to set priorities. One of these I especially like is "Put the Big Rocks in First". If we consider our daily responsibilities as rocks being put into a jar and we put the big ones in first, the smaller things will fill the jar later.

Doing the larger tasks first, finishes them and leaves time for more small ones. If we complete the small things first, the larger ones often go undone and they are usually the most profitable.

Priority setting in business is a vital and fundamental part of the operation. Leaders constantly must adjust them for continual positive productivity. They are never carved in stone, or are unchangeable because customer and associate needs always vary and must be accommodated. It is important for leaders to keep sight of the final outcome and guide procedures in that direction. Part of that precedence setting may require duty delegation or even eliminating the project so the leadership may focus on what only they can complete. Leadership requires decision making with confidence and taking full responsibility for the actions and proper priority setting will accomplish this.

Understanding how to prioritize tasks is a key requirement for successful leadership, particularly within industries such as general retail, construction, and the restaurant business. Team management becomes much easier when you have a well defined idea of the tasks you need to do each day and the best order in which to do them.

Ineffective task management often trickles down to your team members, which results in team communication issues, inefficiencies, and a daily battle to meet deadlines. Read on to find out how to prioritize tasks for a more effective leadership.

Want to make your team communication more efficient?

1. Write Down Your Daily Tasks

Effective task management begins with an action as straightforward as taking two minutes to write down your tasks for the day. It is not efficient to approach task prioritization as an activity you solely conduct mentally.

The physical act of writing things down is powerful because while doing it, your mind tends to intuitively recognize the most important, difficult, and urgent tasks for the day. You can then go further and whittle down this master list of tasks to the two or three most important issues. These are the tasks you can initially concentrate on completing.

2. Tackle Your Most Difficult Tasks First

The idea behind this task prioritization method is to avoid procrastination by tackling the most difficult issues and tasks first. When you sit down and think about all the things you need to do for the day, it's tempting to put the most challenging tasks on the long finger.

However, those challenging tasks tend to lurk in the back of your mind even when you don't prioritize them. The prospect of still having to confront your most difficult tasks can creep into your actions during the more straightforward tasks, and the entire day ends up feeling like an insurmountable mass of objects to overcome.

The beauty of prioritizing the most difficult tasks is that after you complete them, your workload for the rest of the day becomes less stressful because you've gotten the worst tasks out of the way.

Improve team communication and scheduling all in one place. Manage schedules and shift covers without the hassle, stay organized and informed, and save time.

3. Delegate When Appropriate

Any good leader must understand the power and importance of delegation. Assigning a task to someone else does not mean passing the buck of responsibility as a leader. The responsibility for the successful completion of delegated tasks remains with you. However, you have passed on the doing of the task in full recognition that it is impossible for anyone to do it all on their own. Delegation means smart leadership, and it improves task management.

4. Use the Eisenhower Matrix

What better way to draw inspiration for prioritizing tasks than by using a method devised by none other than a former president of the United States: Dwight D. Eisenhower. The Eisenhower Matrix is a priority matrix that prioritizes tasks both by urgency and importance, which leads to four quadrants or categories into which tasks fit.

In essence, if a task is urgent and important, as a leader you need to get it done first. If something is important but not urgent, you pencil it into your schedule. Eisenhower advised delegating tasks that are urgent but less important. The last category identifies tasks that meet the criteria of being both non-urgent and unimportant — remove these tasks from your schedule and from your mind because you shouldn't be doing them.

5. Leverage the Benefits of Mindfulness

Mindfulness is the practice of accepting the present moment and focusing awareness on it. Popularized in western society by Jon Kabat-Zinn, mindfulness has applications in many areas, including leadership. The aim of mindfulness initially seems to conflict with one of the main roles of a leader, which is to look to the future and be prepared for the array of tasks that might arise during the course of a given workday.

However, mindfulness can complement your task prioritization capabilities by informing you of the times in which you feel most productive. By tuning into your feelings and perceptions as you engage in your work, you'll come to realize that a large part of overcoming the challenge of how to prioritize tasks entails simply becoming aware of how you apply your energy at different times.

Aside from these methods for prioritizing tasks, you can use the power of technology to communicate task lists and team schedules to your workers. As a leader, it's imperative to realize that ineffective task prioritization tends to affect all facets of your company, right down to how well your shift workers interact with customers.

Whatever system you use to determine your priorities, remember it is essential to follow it consistently. Bouncing from one item to another never gets anything accomplished and leaves everything only started. Persistence and drive toward a goal achieves it, and distractions will kill it.

Be Committed

If you are a leader, you must gain the trust of your team if you are going to excel at getting results. For some people, trust is gained over a period of time. Sometimes, time is not a commodity you have at your disposal, especially if you have been seconded into a role. Or for example, if you have been brought in to spearhead a project which has a limited time-span. Commitment and the length of time you spend in your role can be a big deal for your followers.

After the retirement of a respected and long-serving senior leader, his new bright-eyed replacement newly selected for the position visited the team. The arrival of the thirty-something female whose career had been fast-paced and widely reported was met with eager anticipation. Not only was she completely different from the outgoing leader; she had a liveliness about her, which together with her highly acclaimed reputation, gave off an air of professional brilliance.

Upon her arrival, her new team were excited, hopeful and welcoming. But the buoyant mood didn't last. Within an hour the atmosphere had changed considerably. In her opening speech, the new leader announced what she hoped to achieve in her time with the team. In the same breath told them her intention was to stay for two years, by which time she would be moving on. The team's optimism was crushed.

In the new leader's mind, she was being upfront and honest with them. In their eyes, she was planning her exit even before she had opened the entrance door. It showed she lacked commitment. The deciding factor for her followers was that the two year term suited the requirements of the larger organization. They concluded it had nothing to do with the leadership task at hand.

Whether you are committed or not may not be in question at all for you as a leader. The question and the doubt raised by longevity in terms of your leadership might be more of an issue for your followers. Followers welcome consistency.

In this fast-paced world, corporate and team leaders come and go. Founder leaders of established companies are more likely to stay and give their followers welcome consistency. There are many stories where founders have exited their leadership roles and their "dream" by selling out and moving on. Only to find the business fails or falters within years, if not months, of their leaving. Given the rate of change both in the business world and as our own goals and dreams change, what role does commitment play in our credibility as a leader?

I believe that whether you are trusted as a committed leader depends on many factors. As a leader, you must fully understand the depth, length and purpose of the commitment required of you. Additionally, you need to be clear about the possibilities of your leadership term being terminated early for you. Also, the circumstances in which you might choose to leave before time. Crucially, in the beginning, middle and end of your term of leadership you plan, communicate and position your intentions.

Principles of Commitment

- As a leader, several principles are relevant in communicating and positioning your commitment in different When appointed for a specific leadership challenge, be clear about your outcomes and be prepared to see it through to the end.

- When appointed for a specific task, determine the part or phase of the task you will lead on, how long that will take, and exactly which outcomes you will be responsible for delivering.

- If you aren't sure you will be reappointed, commit to a dedication to the vision, values and mission of the company while you are there. Be clear about your leadership outcomes during your first term.

- Where you are a founder, a dedication to your own values and vision and a promise to do all within your power to put in place a sustainable plan after you leave.

- A commitment to your followers that you will do the best you can for them while you are there.

circumstances. Commitment is a crucial aspect of your leadership role which gives your followers the certainty they need to be able to develop a relationship with you and grow in trust. You must position your particular leadership commitment so that you can manage expectations.

- A commitment to doing your absolute best no matter how long your term as a leader lasts.

I had no doubt that the new leader described above was committed, albeit for a predetermined period. In retrospect she could have positioned her commitment to two years with a clear vision about her legacy, and what she could do for her followers in that time.

If you lead your team it is vital you position your commitment. If you doubt your commitment to any role, no matter how long it is, then your followers will pick this up. What is true for everyone, whether in a leadership role or not, if you doubt your propensity to stay the course, then simply commit yourself for a day at a time. In that way, you will retain your focus as will those around you.

Believe You Can Do It

Tell me a leader who rejects every suggestion his team gives because he is afraid they cannot make it and I will tell you someone who is not fit to be a leader. Let me quote John Maxwell on how he views positive attitude. In his book, <u>Developing the Leaders Around You</u>, he says, "A positive attitude is one of the most valuables assets a person can have in life." It can help you achieve things that may seem impossible to happen.

As a leader, you will need more than a miracle to make certain things happen. As long as you have the right attitude of looking at things, and on how they have to be done, you can eliminate the miracle part. Most of the time, we become discouraged by how difficult the problems we face are. What we do not know is that it is not really the problems that are difficult to deal with but our attitude towards them. Yes, they may be tough at times and may take a lot of time to solve, but as long as we view them as obstacles that will hinder our way towards our goal, we can never really arrive at the right solution.

Why don't we see these problems as challenges...as something to spice our journey up? Not all roads to success are smooth. Often, there are bumps and humps. If we miss our turn, we might get lost and end up starting all over again. See the big picture. Look beyond the problem. A positive leader will not dwell on a difficult situation and be discouraged by it, but will believe that he can and he ought to surpass it in order to reach his goals. With positive attitude, he never accepts defeat. Instead, he fights the noble battle until the very end.

Believing that you can make something happen is not at all a small thing when you put faith in yourself and believe that you can do it. What the mind says, the body will follow. It is a chain reaction.

When people see that their leader believes and strives hard for accomplishing a task, they will do the same. Imagine, if a single believer can make something happen, then how much more things can a team of believers bring out?

Ok, so you always see the glass half-empty. But you know what? Even if half of the water spills on the floor, it still contains water...and it is half full! Now how can you still see the good things in everything even if you are pessimistic all the time? The answers lie below.

- Keep your mind focused on important things. Set goals and priorities for what you think and do. Visualize practicing your actions and the results you expect from them. Develop an effective strategy for dealing with problems. Concentrate on things that need to be taken seriously; but at the same time, take time to relax and enjoy.

- Keep a list of your goals and actions. Familiarize yourself with things you want to accomplish and with the ways you must undertake to complete them. When you are aware of these things, your body will immediately carry out the actions you need to execute in making these things happen.

- Be detached from the outcome. Life is often compared to a ferris wheel, or a ball, or anything that is round, because of the fact that sometimes we are on the top, and sometimes at the bottom. This only means that there will be times in our lives when some things would not turn out according to what we want them to be. Nevertheless, face them. Do not be annoyed if you do not get what you desire. Do not be discouraged. Do not become too attached to the probable results, but just do your best in everything.

- Balance your desires. We live in a place of opposites and differences, happiness and sadness, pleasure and pain, tears and laughter, love and hate. This is how the cycle of life goes. We can never have all the good things in life at the same time. In wealth, there will always be people who will not be fortunate enough. Measure and moderation is the primary key.

- Be realistic. Make sure that what you want is something possible. Hoping for something to happen, which would never really materialize in real life, will only bring you disappointment. Success cannot be gained overnight, but it can be gained no matter what. Believe and have faith.

- Associate with positive people. In classrooms, work places, or simply anywhere you go where there are groups of people, look for optimistic ones. Associate, hang out, and discuss matters with them. They can help you build self-confidence and self-esteem.

- Ask questions. Asking for or seeking guidance can bring no harm. It does not equate to dumbness and ignorance; rather, it is associated with seeking more information and understanding matters clearly, which is good for you as a leader since you need to learn more things in guiding your people. Remember, with more knowledge, there is also more power.

- Count your blessings. Focus on what you have rather than what you don't have. Positive outcomes emerge when we know we are abundant of this life's blessings. On the other hand, absence of desires will only bring discontentment and disappointment that will only waste our time. So be thankful and appreciative of all the blessings that life has to offer.

- Kiss your worries goodbye. At the end of everyday, before going to sleep, there is no need to keep bad experiences and unhappy moments that had happened during the day. Let them go, throw them out of the window, and kiss them goodbye. Dream sweetly. As a new day unfolds, new hope arises. Keep believing.

Condition Your Mind For Success

You need to be both smart and skilled to lead. But as you look around your organization, you may well find that the best leaders are not always the most technically gifted. If the best leaders are not the most technically competent, then what differentiates the very best from the merely very good?

In the last five years, I have been researching some of the best leaders in business, education, the military, not-for-profit organizations, sports, and beyond to discover their X-factor. During this process, it soon became clear that the best leaders act differently because they think differently. And they all display the same thought biases.

I can call this a mindset, although in practice, a mindset is no more than your thinking habits. As with any habit, we can acquire change, or grow our mental habits with deliberate practice. We may not become a megastar, but even a little practice has a major effect on performance.

My research has uncovered the seven mindsets of success:

High aspirations. Good leaders want to beat the budget and be excellent. For the very best leaders, having high aspirations reaches beyond excellence. They want to change things by finding new ways of working and competing. They meet former U.S. Secretary of State Henry Kissinger's definition of leadership, which is to take people from where they are to where they have not been.

Courage. If you want to change, innovate, and lead, you need courage to break with the old way of doing things. You have to see risk as opportunity. Surprisingly, you can learn courage. Our work with the Royal Marines and British Fire Services showed how they build courage incrementally. What might look like courage to one person is just another day at the office for another. Slowly push your limits, and your ability to manage risk will grow.

Resilience. Research shows that the "best" do not always succeed. But the most successful leaders do not think in terms of failure. Instead, they think that they "have not succeeded ... yet" and use every setback to learn and grow stronger. Crises are the moments of truth that make the best leaders and break others.

Optimism. The positive psychology movement has produced plenty of evidence that being positive is good for your health and longevity. Optimism also is important in the best leaders, for who wants to work for a cynical pessimist? For leaders, optimism is not about "hoping" because, as we know, hope is not a strategy. Instead, optimism is about simple routines: looking to the future and not dwelling on the past; seeing opportunities, not problems; seeking to praise and not to criticize; giving constructive feedback, not negative feedback; and building on strengths and not on weaknesses.

Agency. The best leaders seem to build a reality-distortion field around themselves. They have absolute conviction that they can bend the world to their will. Most of us will be remembered not for our achievements but for our presence. An example that many may have experienced is the way in which a leader's little cloud of gloom can spread like a major depression across teams. The best leaders learn to wear the mask of leadership—they become the leader people want to follow, not the leader people have to follow.

Collaboration. First-time managers have to make the shift from "How do I do this?" to "Who can do this?" In the days of "command and control" organizational structures, that was an easy question to answer - you told a team member to get on with the job. Today, many leaders do not command all the resources they need to succeed; they have to work with partners across and beyond their organizations. That means collaboration is a core, 21st century leadership skill. It is about the art of influence and building networks of trust and support. Aligning agendas makes the organization you work for, work for you.

Growth. The rules of survival and success keep on changing for everyone - from the frontline employee to the supervisor, to the manager of managers, to the CEO. Many leaders fail because they become prisoners of success; they learn a successful formula and stick to it. That's fine as long as the context never changes, but the context is always changing. The best leaders are always learning, growing, and adapting. The growth is not random. They focus on building their strengths and then building a team around them to fill the gaps. As with the collaborative mindset, they know that leadership is no longer about lone heroes changing the world. It is a team sport.

Finally, there is the mindset that appears to come from the dark side:

Ruthlessness. The best leaders are selectively ruthless, and their ruthlessness comes from a complete focus on achieving their mission. They know that when you accept excuses, you accept failure. They also know that success depends on having the best team, they will move team members out quickly if that is required. Ultimately, the fortunes of the organization take precedence over those of the individual. But the best leaders are not psychopaths, they may be unreasonable about goals, but they are flexible about the means and will support the team in reaching its goals.

The best leaders are not always comfortable to work with. They know that the true currency of leadership is not popularity, which leads to compromise and weakness. The true currency is trust and respect, which lead to loyalty and performance. With patience and effort, anyone can build these habits of success.

Stop Caring About What Others Think

Elon Musk announced last year that Tesla would begin laying off about 9% of its workforce. Perhaps unsurprisingly, many employees who had been let go took to Twitter to share their thoughts. And yet, as Bloomberg and Business Insider reported, some former employees expressed surprisingly warm feelings toward Musk and toward his organization.

"I just want to let you know that I really enjoyed working for Tesla," one person tweeted. "No hard feelings about being let go," another wrote. They still believe in the vision and in the mission of the company. It's evidence of the effective way Musk manages his staff.

When Musk made the decision to eliminate some of those positions, he was clearly not making friends, but still, the people who worked for him believed enough in his vision and respected that vision enough that they accepted that this was something that was necessary to do.

I'm using the Tesla firings to illustrate a broader point about leadership. The most successful leaders aren't preoccupied with whether their subordinates like them. Instead, they're focused on doing what's best for the organization. Whether your subordinates love you as a person or whether they hate you as a person, they have to believe in you. Unfortunately, this isn't something most leaders understand.

Competence and warmth are important attributes in a leader but the way to influence and to lead is to begin with warmth. ... Even a few small nonverbal signals - a nod, a smile, an open gesture - can show people that you're pleased to be in their company and attentive to their concerns. That said, be careful not to display too much warmth, at the expense of displaying dominance. It's generally easier to add empathy to dominance than vice versa because the empathetic person may potentially come across as weak.

The most powerful combination is love with some element of fear. In other words, a leader should be invested in people's work experience. But if someone steps out of line or fails to achieve something they said they would, consequences should follow. Leading by fear alone can be an effective strategy but only for a short time period. If your power slips, a lot of people will be coming for your head. If a leader is hated or feared, then people may work hard in some circumstances, but in general they are going to be less mission driven and probably more likely to do just what is required.

Still, simply being adored isn't enough; it's also important to think about why a leader is loved in the first place. A leader should be loved not because they bring doughnuts to the office, but because they treat their employees fairly and in a way that gives those employees a sense that when they work hard, they are rewarded, and that they are working hard in pursuit of some greater collective mission.

If a leader is loved for the right reasons, it's going to be a sign of organizational strength and success. Certain personality types may find it difficult not to be universally loved as a leader. One problem leaders may face in landing on an effective management strategy is that everyone they're managing is different. Some are motivated by strong, dominant leaders; some are motivated by empathetic leaders. Leaders are trying to find a strategy to work on both types of people.

Leaders may struggle to reconcile different people's needs. But they may also struggle with more personal issues. Certain personality types, namely, agreeable and narcissistic - can have a hard time leading effectively. Agreeable people in leadership positions may have difficulty doing things independently of the reaction that people are going to have of them. Specifically, they want to be liked and the idea that doing what is best for the organization may turn some people off is scary. In fact, research suggests that agreeable people are less likely to become top managers in the first place. On the other hand, narcissistic people may take on leadership roles and lash out at people who criticize them or try to take credit for other people's work, which can be demotivating.

As for highly agreeable leaders, I recommend developing personal strategies for, say, giving people news they don't want to hear. Maybe you psych yourself up beforehand with a pep talk. Or you can simply recognize: "I'm an agreeable person." Alienating some people may be necessary, but it doesn't come naturally, and it may feel uncomfortable in the moment.

Many people transitioning into leadership roles are preoccupied with the decision to be liked or feared. But when you actually get into a leadership role, it really does become much more about what you're trying to accomplish with respect to the organization. There's work to be done and spending time worrying what people will think of how you're doing it is generally ineffective.

It takes a really self-confident and resilient individual to make all of these tough judgment calls on a daily basis. But over time, if you make the tough calls with no fudges, if you're fair and don't play favoritism, if you explain your rationale publicly and clearly, if you help soften the blow to the side that doesn't get their way, people will respect you. And it is far better to be respected as a leader than loved.

Set Goals

As a leader, you know one of your biggest responsibilities is to set the organization's direction and help it to achieve goals. You have laid out a mission and a vision for the organization and can talk about it at all levels. But should the goals that come from your level be ultra-specific, or should you create a set of general goals and allow the groups to help you meet them?

The first thing you must do is set a general vision for the organization. Without this general vision, all activity is lost in a cloud of uncertainty. The vision you set should be based in the reality of your environment and should be focused on how the organization will best service its clients. Your vision could be as general as, "to provide the highest level customer service in our industry, every time, with every customer." But at least you can be assured that each person, whether internal or external, will use that vision as an overarching theme for everything they do.

You have set the overall vision, but what about the goals within that vision? Is it up to you to create specific goals? In two words, yes and no. You must create some frame for the work that is going to occur over the next quarter, year, or even five years. For example, one of your goals for the organization may be to "increase market share to 50% over the next five years." Is the goal reasonable? Can the organization do it? Do you have the right people in place to execute the goal? If you answer yes to each question, you've got to sit back and try to let it happen. When it does, celebrate the results. When it doesn't, obtain input from the organization as to how they can be better prepared the next time. One of the other ways to help reach goals is to create a "stretch" environment, where celebration occurs for the increments of success. For example, you could say, "increase market share to 47% this year, 48% next year, 49% in 2021, and 50% in 2022." Each time the group hits a target, celebrate it as a step in the right direction.

The hardest part of this mentality is learning to curb your urge to be an "armchair quarterback." You should know how each group within the organization can help achieve the general goals you've set. You should also hold them accountable for the goals that their leader will set for them. But you've got to let them figure out how they can help the organization hit its goals, and then let them run with it. In other words, make sure the leaders of each group know how to set direction on a smaller scale. Make sure those leaders know how to select and hire the right people to get the job done. And make sure you all stand out of their way when they get their momentum.

In this same manner, you must be aware of how the execution of your general goals will change based on the groups and the internal and external factors affecting them. Let them help you figure out how to let the goals evolve. Show them that you and your leadership team are open to suggestion, and that the people who do the work are the ones who generally have the best ideas on execution. The strategy you set, those general goals you lay out, should allow the groups to maneuver, use their expertise, and come up with new and improved ways of doing things.

By showing the organization that you are open to new ideas, you are encouraging the removal of traditional boundaries. When you set general goals for the organization, the groups will have to learn how they interact with other groups in order to keep the organization producing. In many organizations, especially large corporations, the walls around groups may have built up inadvertently and over lengths of time. Most of the time these walls are based on comfort or fear, and the idea that the status quo is the best situation. As you show that you and your leadership team have removed walls, other groups will learn this as well. Encourage groups to have cross-functional discussions on the execution of your general goals. In this environment, groups will maneuver to achieve, but you will find that they may start maneuvering with each other, as well.

Set general goals and allow the organization to execute them. You will see creativity, less boundaries, and an overall move to achieve your goals together.

Take Action

Leaders in any field are often recognized for being the first to do something, or perhaps for having achieved the biggest or most difficult feat. Sometimes their very leadership, and ultimately their branding, is identified by having achieved.

Yet so often success or progress is held back by the forces that conspire to hinder a leader's success; such progress being compromised by the interruptions, compromises and insecurities that hold leaders back from achievement.

Military history abounds with accounts of leaders whose mission failed after stretching their forces too far due to lack of support, resources, or back up; business lore resounds with records of organizations that foundered due to being under-capitalized, under-trained, or unprepared in some way; and sporting history reveals the poignant accounts of athletes who experienced great disappointment and ignominy, even within sight of victory, due to being physically or psychologically unprepared.

The annuls of history also record the stories of great leaders who possessed that intuitive quality of vision mixed with perspective; who saw opportunity and determined to run with it; who intuitively calculated that they could go where no one had gone before; who weighed up the odds, believed in themselves and their teams and set out to achieve the impossible; who refused to accept the negativity and doubt of their skeptics, and went on to achieve greatness, establishing new records, standards and normals.

Great leaders know that whilst achievement usually depends on proper planning and preparation in advance, the single most important criteria is to take action; and this may mean taking massive, unrestrained and uncompromised action in the face of doubters and opposition.

These great leaders are generally prepared physically, in some cases financially, and in all cases mentally, to act when opportunity presents itself. Once they gain a vision of what they want, they immediately set about preparing, resourcing and training in the expectation that their day will come. Never, ever will they be guilty of facing opportunity and lamenting that fact that if only they were ready; they are permanently ready in expectation.

Without exception they refuse to accept that it can't be done. Without exception they refuse to delay, stall or procrastinate when they see the chance to achieve their goal. These men and women exercise initiative in the face of complacency or when others think it need not be done. They take action in the face of difficulty, when others say it can't be done. They act in the face of mediocrity, when naysayers say it should not be done. And they step up to the occasion when onlookers say it is not necessary or the right time to do it. These people will not delay simply because some part of their process is not quite ready. They are not ones to wait until each one of their ducks are lined up. They realize that perfect opportunities rarely, if ever, come and that the time to act is now.

These leaders will not accept, nor will they give excuses as to why, action should not be taken and invariably live by the philosophy that today is the day, that tomorrow never comes. They inherently seize the moment. Great leaders such as these fully understand that fear of the unknown, of failure or of criticism is inherently normal, yet should never be accepted as a reason to hold back. Fear is something to be harnessed, not something that restricts us.

Master A Skillset And Use It

If you have found yourself in a leadership role, congratulations! This is a huge turning point in your career. You are probably feeling a mix of excitement, nervousness and fear. Those feelings are perfectly normal and healthy. In fact, if you were going into your new role as cool as a cucumber, I would be nervous for you.

Why? Because leading people is a challenge. No one can be ready for what is about to happen when you start to lead others. You cannot predict what your team will throw at you, so take the time in advance to nail down the following skills before you step into the leadership role (if you're already in that role, it is okay, it won't hurt to keep reading).

1. Values

Values define what you do and why you do it. If you are unclear on what your core values are, figure them out (this may help) and come back to this article. Once you are clear on your values, stick with them. If you do, your role as a leader will become more straightforward. From your values comes your mission and your vision. They have to be aligned, as they will provide your foundation for the future. Values are core beliefs and define your attitude, relationships and environment. Know your values, and know where you stand. This will put everything you do and say into context.

49

2. Self-awareness

I hear a lot of people say that the most effective leaders have excellent communication skills. True, but I would go one step further and say that most effective leaders are extremely self-aware. You cannot communicate effectively to everyone if you aren't. Knowing that I was a big picture thinker, who did not focus on small details, allowed me to recognise other people's styles and to do the following:

Ajust my communication style when dealing with key stakeholders who were more detailed oriented (i.e., a big picture business pitch to someone who can't dream without seeing the figures will fall flat every single time.)

By taking the time to know yourself, you will have a great understanding of what you bring to the team, and what you need to build up in others. Do not try to be great at everything; hone in on your key skills and master them. I was lucky to be introduced to a self-awareness profile which was combined with regular coaching sessions. I used the profile tool on my whole team, which was a game changer for me. If you have resources like this available to you, take advantage of them now. If you do not, keep a look out for what is out there so you can start immediately.

3. Good communication

In my opinion, the key to good communication is a balance of the following: 20% effectively getting your message across, and 80% being a good listener. I always encourage open lines of communication and recommend this to everyone. Remember: there is a big difference between saying this and practising it. If you are going to have an "open door" policy, you have to listen and act on what you hear. If you cannot act immediately, then communicate that back, and ensure your team understands why you cannot. The worst feeling an employee can have is one of feeling that they are not being heard. It automatically slams your "open door" policy shut.

Most leadership experts agree that the most important role of a leader is to effectively communicate the organization's mission and vision. Every member of your team should understand how his or her role plays a part in the bigger picture of the business. There is no "one size fits all" approach to being an effective leader. It all comes down to who you are as a person, and who you have in your team. But you can be a step ahead of the game when you know your values, know yourself and know how to communicate and listen effectively. Don't fall into the management trap. Inspire and enable your team by acting as a true leader.

4. Goal Orientation

Energetically focusing efforts on meeting a goal, mission, or objective. Some examples include demonstrating persistence in overcoming obstacles to meet and accomplish goals, taking necessary calculated risks to achieve results, acting with a sense of urgency, recognizing opportunities, and acting independently.

5. Self-Management

Demonstrating self-control and an ability to manage time and priorities. Some examples are effectively managing emotions and reactions, effectively managing time and priorities to complete initiatives on time, striving for balance in life, continuously improving, and using logic and reason to develop rational alternatives to current assumptions.

Become Obsessed

Many individuals become involved in positions of leadership, but very few become truly great leaders. Great leadership is never a one-time, or overnight occurrence, but rather requires a continuous commitment to doing whatever is necessary, in order to achieve the results desired. In many ways, this commitment must become a sort of positive obsession, because to accomplish what others have not, is often challenging, with numerous obstacles and obstructions along the way. The greatest leader keeps his focus constantly on the target, which is his goal in terms of making a vital vision approach reality. Pat Riley, one of the most successful and visionary professional basketball coaches and executives of all times said, "To have long term success as a coach or in any position of leadership, you have to be obsessed in some way."

1. Perhaps the greatest roadblock for successful leaders, is to remain upbeat and positive at all times, constantly searching for ways to improve and enhance their organization. While lesser leaders may try once or twice, and then often give up or shift gears if they are unable to achieve a goal, the successful ones remain focused, never giving up on those goals he feels most crucial. This is somewhat of an obsession, because being a great leader can never be a one time endeavor, but requires absolute

commitment, and a spirit of prioritizing his organization. These leaders have a feeling and an emotional attachment for an organization that never diminishes simply because of challenges, obstacles, opposition, or the negativity of others.

2. The late General Robert Shira, who was not only a General, but also the United States Dental Surgeon General, as well as a Dean and a Provost, modestly proclaimed that his accomplishments were possible because he outlived his contemporaries. In reality, he achieved because he was talented, intelligent, spoke beautifully, and most importantly, placed whatever duty he was presently responsible for as his highest priority, refusing to fail. Some might consider that somewhat of an obsession.

An obsession can be either be positive or negative, depending upon what it is, and how it is used. When it is negative, it saps a person of his energy and takes away focus from what should be priorities. On the other hand, when an obsession is for something positive, it is an energy supplement, focusing on priorities, and enabling someone to persist and persevere when others give up. The greatest and most successful leaders did not achieve their success because they never had failures, but rather that they did not permit those events to impact them negatively. Rather, they gained and became better and stronger after each adversity.

Start With Small Daily Habits

If you make your bed every morning you will have accomplished the first task of the day. It will give you a small sense of pride and it will encourage you to do another task and another and another. And by the end of the day that one task completed will have turned into many tasks completed.

Starting out with a small accomplishment helps you tackle bigger things throughout the day. It helps you have the right frame of mind from the get go.

Science tells us that there is good reason to make small changes to our daily habits rather than trying to change our daily routines all at once. Tiny habits rely less on willpower and motivation and more on redesigning your life little by little, so over time these small shifts create dramatic results.

Here are some of the daily habits of top performers and the small steps you can take to incorporate them into your life today:

1. Practice Gratitude

Taking time to focus on what they are grateful for and to express thanks to those around them is one of the habits of many highly successful people (think: Tim Ferriss and Paul DeJoria).

Practicing gratitude can help you become happier, improve relationships and even improve your brain. This habit takes a minimum amount of time and resources to put into motion. All it takes is a mental shift. Make sure practicing gratitude becomes a habit by writing in a journal each night before you go to sleep, in one sentence, what you were grateful for that day.

Two in One: Journal. The one sentence gratitude journal actually builds two habits at once: practicing gratitude and journaling (another habit of many successful leaders).

2. Exercise

I know this one might seem like a big change for many people. But in any book about the daily habits of top performers it can't be avoided. It is reported that 76% of self-made millionaires do at least 30 minutes of aerobic exercise daily. Barack Obama, Mark Zuckerberg, and yes, the 5:00 a.m. waking Richard Branson, have all discussed the importance of exercise to their overall performance and productivity. Exercise is not only good for your body, it is good for your brain. And it provides another way to achieve a sense of accomplishment that can waterfall throughout your day.

If beginning an exercise regime seems overwhelming, start small. Walk. Just walk. A great article on developing a walking habit can be found here. If walking isn't an option for you, find another small way to incorporate movement into your daily routine.

Two in One: Read. By far, one of the most common habits of highly successful people is reading. While you might not be able to read for three hours a day like Mark Cuban, you can listen to audiobooks while you exercise.

Pick books that help you gain knowledge in the area you work, gain insight into the world and yourself, or provide a different perspective. For some great book recommendations from one of the greatest living entrepreneurs, check out Bill Gates' book blog.

3. Meditate

Oprah Winfrey and Arianna Huffington are both big proponents of meditation. Meditation has been scientifically shown to decrease anxiety and improve cognition, among many other benefits.

In fact, Huffington argues that meditation can be good for the bottom line, saying, "Stress-reduction and mindfulness do not just make us happier and healthier, they are a proven competitive advantage for any business that wants one."

Newcomers to meditation may worry that it will require a lot of time and energy, but it doesn't have to. Meditating for as little as 10 minutes a day can help enhance your ability to focus.

Two in One: Drink Water. Drinking water can help you stay fresh and alert. Use the end of your meditation time as a signal to drink a glass of water. Incorporating one habit into another is called "habit stacking" and it can help make a new habit stick.

Bonus Tip. If you're starting to lose focus at work, consider taking a 10-minute break to meditate. Double up the good habit and have a glass of citrus water afterwards. You'll feel the difference.

Stay On Track With Your Goals

When you're not on track with your business, you will find you will not reach your goals and you will not grow. When this happen you will find you get discouraged and do not want to continue on with your business. This is not a good thing whether you use your business for a solid income to support your family or you use it for extra cash to do the things you want to do.

There are a number of things you can do to stay on track with your business, but if you do not know what they are you cannot make sure to get them done. With that being said, it is important to make sure you have what you need to do them and how to make it happen. Below are tips to help you do just that so your business will reach success.

The first thing you need to do is create a list of goals. If you do not have goals in place you will not be able to grow because you will not know what to do. You may not have the need or want to grow at first, but once you begin to see it happen you will want it. Goals need to be business related, but on the flip side of that, you need personal goals that are tied to the business goals so you will know why you want growth.

Once your goals are created you need to figure out what it is going to take to make sure you reach them. Figure out step by step what it will take and how much time you will need to get them accomplished. Once you have done this with every goal, you are ready to take it one step further and put it into action. This will include adding the steps to your to do list and scheduling the time to make it happen.

When your step by step goals are put into place, you are ready to put your game plan into action. You may find if your goals are a bit higher and more difficult to achieve, you may not be able to make it happen. If that is the case, then you need to change your goals a bit or you may need to outsource part of the entire goal in order to make it happen.

When you create and work your goals you will find it will be a lot easier to manage your business and stay on track as well. Whether you work your goals completely by yourself, or if you outsource certain tasks, you will see growth when you do and that is what you set out to achieve when you plan your business and stay on track.

Optimize Your Environment

Several studies have been completed on the ways to optimize your work environment and the benefits of optimization. Studies focus on topics ranging from identifying with the place you work, the type of furniture in the office, to the use of color and lighting. These give you a wide range of possibilities to increase health and productivity in the office. Though the options are plentiful, here I provide you with a few tips on how to ensure an efficient, productive and healthy work environment for everyone.

Refresh Your Workspace Arrangement

Many people spend hours sitting at their desk working on computers, and the typical set up is a standard desk and a chair. However, there are alternatives. For example, many people find their productivity increases when they use an adjustable standing desk that allows them to stand or sit as they choose. Another option is for team members to replace chairs with aerobic balls. These can have a positive effect on health, posture and thus on productivity.

Ask Your Team: "When do you work best?"

Some individuals are morning people, while others are more productive in the afternoon. Allow individual team members to figure out when they are at their most effective and to plan their schedule accordingly. When possible, flexi-hours and four-day work-weeks can go far to increase your team's performance.

Decoration and Lighting

A colorful workspace can boost motivation, as can a lighting scheme. What's more, studies have found that rounded furniture creates a more productive work environment than angular furniture does. Such matters may seem trivial, but if the office is going to be filled with furniture anyway, it's much better to choose furniture that adds to, rather than detracts from, efficiency.

Plants and Artwork

Plants, too, are an excellent way to build a warm, inviting work atmosphere. They give the office a sense of life beyond the day-to-day tasks of business. The less sterile and the more alive an office feels, the more productive and happier your team will be. Artwork with inspiring and motivational words can also create a backdrop that works on a subconscious level to push your team toward greater innovation and efficiency.

Keep Things Positive

Studies show that people work better in positive environments. If you want to optimize your workspace, make sure that the energy amongst the team is as positive as possible. If you notice a negative air in the office, take steps to rectify the situation through conflict resolution, rewriting of rules, or any other measures you deem necessary. Have an open ear for team members' concerns so that they, too, have a say in what their positive work environment looks like. With a focus on positive energy, you will also notice an increase in efficiency and a greater willingness to engage with the work.

Exploit Available Technology

Our modern world continues to see rapid advances in technology, and this can be a great boon for your work environment. Take time to learn about the latest technologies and how you can implement them in your workplace. Whether it is a new accounting program designed to streamline the process or new keyboards tailored to the ergonomic needs of your team members, even the smallest technological advances can be a significant benefit to your company.

Optimize with Your Team

As you strive to optimize your work environment, remember that a tyrannical leader, even with the best intentions, does more harm than good. Give your team members a voice in the process; after all, it is as much their work environment as it is yours. Doing your best to pull your team into the process of optimization makes your job easier and the new measures that much more palatable to them.

Boost Productivity

Often when leaders talk about increasing productivity, what they really mean is that they think people should work harder. This is not a very motivating concept because what they are actually saying is that they do not believe their teams are working hard enough. This actually has the opposite effect, and it demotivates teams. It just isn't good leadership.

Good leaders understand that there is a big difference between working hard and being more productive. Asking people to just work harder is the lazy leader's way of trying to increase output. Instead, good leaders ensure that their teams have the right tools, resources, and training to be effective.

This means that leaders should analyze everything that they do and eliminate tasks that add little or no value or detract from the actual goal. Leaders need to focus on finding ways to work smarter, not harder. And remember, there is a physical limit to the number of hours in a day.

When leaders take this approach, they will find that their teams are more motivated and appreciate their leadership. When these workers see that their efforts are turned directly into output, they are much more prepared to increase their effort. They become inspired, which is the goal of all leaders - to inspire their teams.

People want to be successful. As leaders, we need to put our teams in the position where they can be as successful as possible. Once we have done that, then our job becomes easy. It is then merely a question of recognizing and praising the increased output of our employees. When teams are focused on the wrong things, it does not matter how much harder they work, neither the leader nor the worker will see any benefit. Instead, it will just lead to frustration and demotivation.

Giving work a higher purpose

I am often asked: "What's the best way to increase employee engagement?"

I think there are many answers, but the first and most effective leadership practice is to give the work a higher purpose, if possible. We all want to feel that we performed a great day's work and really added value.

Case in point: When I worked at DHL, the business manager told the team that the real purpose of "Improving On-Time Delivery Program" was not about improving customer satisfaction, reducing penalties, or increasing productivity. Instead, the real purpose of the program was to ensure that kids got their birthday presents on their birthday, and that patients received their medication when they needed it. This gave the work a higher purpose. You could see employee engagement visibly rise within the group. Not only did the team know what they were doing, they understood why.

Another way to increase engagement is to escalate employee involvement in the decision-making process. As the saying goes, "No involvement, no commitment."

If people feel as though they had a part in the decisions, they will feel more involved in the project. Their thinking shifts. Now, it is their project rather than something that has been predetermined and they have no chance of shaping it.

A good leader can also increase engagement through the way that he interacts with his team. If leaders keep their distance and manage through a "command and control" style, they will have a negative effect. Whereas a leader who is open and close to his team, where the team feels they are working with the leader rather than for the leader, will instill significantly more engagement in his team.

The better your team understand the goals, the approach, and the reasoning, the more engaged they will be. If they are unsure of the what, why, and how, then it is very difficult to engage. While there are many other techniques to increase engagement, I do feel that these are the most powerful and should be explored first.

Self-Discipline

Self-discipline, resilience, and integrity all go hand in hand. But in a much broader sense, the discipline that strong leaders demonstrate reflects much more than mere self-control.

Disciplined leaders must be able to consistently make decisions that are clear headed, informed, and conclusive. Their response to difficult and stressful situations is thoughtful and purposeful, never random or subjective, particularly in emotionally charged situations. Objectives are communicated clearly and unambiguously. This is not always an easy thing to do, which is why self-discipline has such a profound impact on those around us. To borrow (and modify) a quote from the world of sports... "Adversity doesn't build character, it reveals it." A firm, definite, and decisive leader demonstrates grace under pressure, very clearly reinforcing the perception that he or she is in complete control of both the situation and his or her own emotions.

While disciplined leaders are by necessity decisive, they must at the same time exercise sound judgment. Emotions run high in times of crisis. Most people intuitively look for someone to "do something" in emergencies. It requires great discipline to think before responding. Any situation that requires action, whether a crisis, conflict, or everyday business decision, necessitates a thoughtful and measured response from a leader. Knowledge and experience are necessary, even crucial. But like a sword, they are only as effective as the person wielding them.

Leaders can, and should be, flexible when appropriate. However, it is one thing to compromise on matters of preference, it is quite another to compromise on matters of principle. Principles are rooted in personal doctrine or institutional values, and are a specific basis for conduct or management. Preferences are simply a matter of who controls non-essentials, and are driven by experience and familiarity.

Strong, disciplined leaders understand this difference. Unfortunately, in a world where the boundaries of morality and ethics are deemed malleable and subject to individual interpretation, the concept of 'right' and 'wrong' becomes driven by convenience and preference lacks any principled bearing. As a consequence, the line between principle and preference is grayed. Principles are compromised for sake of appeasement or through capitulation to the path of least resistance.

It takes courage to draw a line in the sand, to stand up for what you believe. Some consider this to be close minded or prejudicial, even intolerant. One thing is for sure, those in positions of influence weaken themselves as leaders whenever they compromise their principles. Whether in the business world or politics, it is rare to find everyone in agreement. This is not to say that leaders should not be appropriately questioned. Convictions that cannot be reasonably defended, should be rightfully challenged.

Values vary and people come to different conclusions and form different beliefs. It requires strength of conviction and great discipline to stay the course when faced with temptation to concede or compromise principles. However, people are far more willing to follow a principled and disciplined leader, even one with whom they disagree. By contrast, no one will follow a leader they do not trust or in whom they have no faith, or in leaders who fail to be true to themselves and the principles on which they claim to stand.

Control Your Emotions

Driven by their emotions, bad leaders react quickly to situations often without worrying about the facts or the repercussions of their actions, believing that they can always show good emotional intelligence by apologizing later. Unfortunately, it doesn't work like that.

Leaders cannot just react, they need to be calm and show composure, even under pressure. They need to show consideration, be perceived as thoughtful and taking the facts into account, and then giving measured responses. You cannot just lash out at people or situations.

When you do that, it sets the tone for the organization, and it can create a stressful environment. An environment where people choose not to pass on information or bad news, because they fear that it will be the messenger who will get shot.

When we disrupt the information flow, it creates all kinds of issues, it can lead to you not being up to date or informed about what is going on, it can mean that you missed the opportunity to address a critical situation before it became a catastrophe.

Don't confuse being emotional with emotional intelligence either, they are definitely not the same thing. I remember one former boss trying to tell me that by wearing his heart on his sleeve and letting people see his emotions that this was the height of emotional intelligence. He also believed that with passion comes emotion and that it was a good trade-off, and therefore being emotional should be tolerated.

Emotions are a good thing, but they need to be channeled correctly, they cannot be allowed to run unchecked and just erupt at any moment. That just makes you appear to be volatile and volatility is not a great leadership quality. Also, if people know you can easily be baited, and that they can get you to react emotionally and lash out, they can look to use this against you and undermine your career.

One of the smartest people I have ever worked with never achieved their full potential because everyone knew that if you challenged him aggressively, he could not handle it and that they would have a bit of meltdown. Given that the competition for jobs at the top is fierce, they were often challenged by other managers to highlight this failing to take them out of contention for any promotions that they were applying for. Yes it is unfair, and I can honestly say it is not something I participated in or condoned, but that did not stop it from limiting their careers.

There is a subtle but paramount difference between reacting and responding. Reacting is when we unconsciously experience an emotional trigger and behave in an unconscious way that causes us to express or relieve that emotion. This may cause us to chastise someone because we are irritated that we have been interrupted.

However, when we respond, we notice how we are feeling, and we consciously decide how we will respond. In the case of the interruption, we could politely let them know we are busy and to come back in 10 or 15 minutes.

Discover what your emotional triggers are, so that you can look to prepare yourself to better manage your reaction. When you know that someone has started to touch on one of these sensitive subjects, you understand your feelings, and learn the subtle warning signs, so you know that you are starting to react rather than respond.

And failing that, be prepared to grit your teeth and count to 10 before you respond. It might not look stylish but words spoken can never be taken back. They may be forgiven, but they are never forgotten.

Don't be driven by your emotions, leaders need to be seen to be calm, considered and thoughtful at all times, as it build trust and can reduces stress in difficult situations. The tendency to over react, or letting your emotions get the better of you, can be used to undermine you credibility, and limit your opportunities.

Don't Get Distracted By 'Shiny Objects'

One of the greatest challenges of leadership is managing time, a limited resource that has to be used with the utmost care and consideration.

As the saying goes, there are "only so many hours in a day", and the leader must be able to stay focused on those tasks and activities that truly matter.

That task is complicated by the daily presence of many distractions that the leader must avoid, lest putting themselves (and their company) in jeopardy.

There are three distractions that are particularly dangerous:

The "Bright Shiny Object" – It is a new product, a new project, or a new partner that catches your eye. It sounds really cool, and there is probably a lot of buzz going on about it in the corridors, and probably even in the business pages. The problem is, it is not really right for the company, or it is a very long shot for success. But its really cool! So you devote a lot of time on it, at the expense of other, more viable and profitable things.

The "Black Hole" – The company has committed a lot of money to a particular project and you are trying to guide it to a successful conclusion. Trouble is, about 25% of the way in, it becomes pretty

74

clear that things aren't going well (and you are going to be over budget to boot), and you face a decision – pull the plug now (with all the resulting hand wringing and blame), or, ask for more money and trudge on. You choose the latter, and enter the black hole – pressing dangerously on in the hope that somehow, someway it will get pulled out in the end.

The "Fire Drill" – The phone rings, and it's your boss. He saw a blog post yesterday from an unhappy customer – it was a pretty ugly one - but when you dug into it the day before it appeared to be an isolated case that could be routinely handled by your customer service staff, and you had set up a protocol for cases exactly like this one. Your boss looks at it differently. It is a complete breakdown of customer service that needs an extensive review and accounting. You then start the fire drill which consists of two days of phone calls, e-mails, and meetings involving many members of your team, devoted to that single blog post.

These kind of distractions can be avoided. It is all a matter of leadership perspective, that ability to take a step back, and "see" the bigger picture. It also requires something else that is even more essential – courage.

The courage to put down a bright shiny object in the face of all that "coolness." The courage to stop a black hole project dead in its tracks and take the heat. And, the courage to tell your boss you will not conduct a fire drill because of a single and isolated incident.

Perspective and courage are your best tools for time management - use them well, and wisely. And one more thing, be aware of that smartphone too, lots of bright shiny objects there.

Conclusion

Brian Tracy, famous speaker, author, and trainer, has worked with more than 1,000 companies in the last 25 years and he has worked with every type of leader. The success of your company, the success of your family, and your own personal success is all determined by leadership abilities. And, guess what? These abilities can all be learned. You can become a leader by thinking and acting like a leader. Leadership is about taking action. Take specific actions that make a difference in your life and others. Start practicing the discussed tips to become a successful leader today. Practice, practice, practice.

The final secret. Every leader started as a follower. Everyone at the top started at the bottom. There are no limits to what you can accomplish except for the limits you place on your own thinking. So, get out there and just do it.

To your success and dreams.

Made in the USA
Columbia, SC
18 September 2020